CHAGALL

Text by
WERNER SCHMALENBACH

Translated from the German by
M. LEDIVELEC

CROWN PUBLISHERS, INC. ⌄ NEW YORK

LIST OF ILLUSTRATIONS

COVER PLATE

THE WEDDING

1928. Oil, $58^1/_4'' \times 32''$. LeRay Berdeau Collection, Palm Beach, U.S.A.

Chagall learned to appreciate the bouquet in France. It became for him symbolic of that loved country and a token for loving and being loved. Here it spread over the bridal pair in the moonlight night, soaring up from their hearts to the sky from which the angel descends to quiet music. On the hillock in the background is another angel, dancing rather theatrically and rather pathetically, to give the blessing of heaven on these lovers. Their embrace is shy and awkward, the symbolism of flowers and angels is naïve, naïve as the romantic moon, mirrored in the river and bathing the whole picture in its blue light.

MARC CHAGALL

Chagall and the Twentieth Century: what a fortunate, what a blessed encounter! If it is true that every artist only awakes and reveals himself when the historical moment is ripe for his appearance, we must recognise a special dispensation of Providence in this meeting. We can speak of Providence or Chance, as we like, it is in any case not a compelling necessity at work, such as brings out a Picasso or a Klee in such an age as ours. For while these artists are born in an epoch characterised by the historic moment, Marc Chagall's cradle was outside the realms of history as measured in centuries, decades or even shorter periods. Here was no son of the Age, called by that Age to practise his art. He grew up, rather, in a world in which scarce an echo was heard of such a call, a world buried for centuries in a twilight of indifference, unlit by time or history, wrapped in its age-long traditions. So that it was in verity a coincidence and not the outcome of historic necessity. Two worlds far apart came together and set off the spark. Natural as this encounter may seem in retrospect, it might easily have never occurred. Among a thousand possibilities, it was just a matter of law that Chagall and the 20th century could merge.

Each was waiting for the other: Chagall for the Century into which he had been born and the 20th Century for him, whom it had not yet found. Each was prepared for the other by age-long separate processes.

Seeking for an analogy, one might quote the extraordinary emergence of the Douanier Rousseau who in the same way only achieved prominence because the Age was prepared for such a phenomenon and welcomed him. But in that case the encounter was one-sided in its acceptance and its result. Rousseau did not leave the limits of his narrow circle, not even when the Century, fascinated, turned its eyes on him. Chagall, on the other hand, was both a benefactor to his Century and the recipient of its favours. What made this possible was certainly the special quality of his Art. But an equally potent cause was the particular artistic aspirations of the Age, which found recognition and satisfaction at the hands of this newcomer from a distant land.

It would be idle to speculate whether Chagall's encounter with any other century would have been so fruitful. From the human point of view this is perhaps not so unthinkable, for, if it was the characteristic urge of this period to recapture the origins of human existence that found such wonderful fulfilment in Chagall, this urge was not unknown to previous epochs. Indeed a yearning for the lost paradise of his origins is perhaps a basic feature of man's nature and this yearning has found forms of expression—mythological, philosophic and artistic—from the earliest times down to the civilisation of the 19th and 20th centuries. But no period before our own was so prepared for the marriage of artistic values, form and style with dateless or pre-historic manifestations of art. Moreover, it would always have been felt necessary to consider art outside the limits of the naturalistic. This necessity was first apparent round 1900 when, together with a growing artistic development the horizon of our aesthetic experiences was extended in so unexpected a way: the art of the oldest civilisations, that of uncivilised peoples and even peasant-art all became of interest. These previously despised manifestations now attracted the most passionate attention.

It was then that this youth of barely twenty from furthest Russia appeared on the scene. He seemed to have sprung from a province akin to primitive art—to wit that of Russo-Jewish folk-lore and he was therefore welcomed as a naive and guileless incarnation of all that the moderns were striving to recover.

Nevertheless Chagall was not an artist of the type common in every folk-lore: one among many nameless ones producing anonymous works of art, all confined within the strict convention they have inherited, never overstepping its borders. His world had known no art, for the God of his Forefathers forbade all pictures and, apart from ritualistic subjects any portraiture or descriptive art were things unknown and basically impossible. But his irrepressible although still childish pictorial urge led Chagall to cross the ordained boundary. Wrapped as he was in the spiritual atmosphere of his origins, with the religiosity of the Hasidhim group and the laws and customs of his race in the homely world of Witebsk, by the mere fact that he began to paint he had abandoned it all. And from the start it could not be peasant art that he followed—he must accept the personal responsibility and give it his own name. Thus, the barriers being overthrown, he took his art with him out into the world. His good fortune was that this world beyond his own purview was historically ready for him. Due to this, he could enter the " Period " to its advantage and his own.

He brought to Europe a folk-lore that was no folk-lore. His art was only the reflection of folk-lore. For attachments counted with him and even if his idiom was or became a different one, the subject and tone of his pictures left no doubt of his spiritual origins. It was naïveté and yet no naïveté which found expression in his art. For while he carried in his heart the world of his origin, his childhood and his faith and something of his early outlook on men and things, he was not altogether unaware of artistic forms and norms. In matters of art, he needed a spark, a seed

3

from without. In this respect he was open to all impressions which might help him to find himself.

It is natural that his artistic visions should be awakened by new subjects and new forms. But these visions were still subjected to the laws of his original world-perception. They preserved an irrationality which for him was quite logical and therefore in no way opposed to reason even when they allowed a somewhat weak artistic rationale to take control. Nevertheless, the encounter with western art, first in Petersburg, then more strongly in Paris and Berlin, was full of danger for him. He might easily have succumbed to the manifold influences which now pressed in upon him. When they did not suit his needs, he rejected them, thanks to the hidden strength of his ambition. He had already rejected in Petersburg what was antagonistic to him in western modern art. But he recognised with all the more enthusiasm the opportunities which Paris was offering him.

The drama of the adoption by Chagall of the " Art of the Period " is played visibly—palpably—before our eyes. His contribution, at first sight, seems to be no more than a naive naturalism, remarkable only for an unusual power of expression. It is reminiscent of the artistic talk of adolescents, free from formal control, objective but still somewhat clumsily descriptive. But it would be wrong to speak only of naturalism, of which the artist is in no sense a master. On the other hand, it would be equally wrong to try to recognise at this stage an explicit formal intention. The naturalism is naive but has not yet reached its goal and its lack of skill and helplessness lends it the character of a personal idiom. It is a naturalism all the better adapted to depiction and description in that it has not yet reached perfection and, just by this fact, has kept something of the irrational and expressive character of all real narrative art. It is indeed a pre-naturalistic style, but more on the lines of the naturalistic than the definitely un-naturalistic. From the beginning this idiom has the dreamy, tender tone which can clarify the barest subjects and this tone remains typical of Chagall. Men, beasts, objects, spaces—all are naively presented just as they really are without either a personal evaluation or one dictated by tradition and convention.

His initial contact with the Conventional art of the period—first in the School of Art of his provincial home-town Witebsk, then in St. Petersburg—did not launch Chagall on the stream of academic naturalism. He adhered rather to his childish amateur style. But he raised this not quite developed naturalism to an unusual expressivity. If his hesitation to accept its logical implications had formerly been due to the limitations of his own naturalism, it now hardened into a conscious and intentional renunciation. This was his first decisive revulsion against the orthodox school. From now on he consciously foreshortens, wilfully ignores the laws of natural construction, exaggerates the expressivity of figures and backgrounds and even distorts colours, but always in the direction of heavier, darker tones. But with all this the figures keep their amateurish character. His pictures recall the crude daubs with which street-singers advertise their performance or vendors their booths at the annual Fair. Only his strong human feeling and the sensitive colouring raise Chagall's work well above such amateurish art.

Chagall arrived in Paris in 1910. The very next day he visited the Salon des Independants, focus of the young revolutionary Art of the capital. Although he was also impressed by the Louvre, it was the encounter with the new movement that proved decisive. He was soon accepted in both the artistic and literary groups of the Avant Gardists of the pre-war years. He made friend with the leading progressive painters and poets of 1910—especially the poets. He meets Lèger, Modigliani, Soutine, Gleizes, Metzinger, La Fresnaye—and of the literary world Blaise Cendrars, Apollinaire, Canudo. He becomes familiar with Cubism, particularly in its coloured « Orphistic » variation, which attains supremacy under Delaunay. When the poet Apollinaire introduces him to Herwarth Walden, president of the Berlin gallery « Der Sturm » and editor of the periodical of the same name, Chagall soon becomes known in Germany as a leading representative of young international art. An enthusiastic, overwhelming world of artistic feeling flows over him and he eagerly surrenders to it. While refusing to be turned aside from the path of his personal art, he seeks to identify himself with the new forms of expression which are gaining favour. So it is that the process which started in his home town of Witebsk is now in full play under the glaring light and cross fire of by-words and « programmes ». In an astonishingly short time Chagall has become one of the most promising exponents of the Art of the Avant Garde. Indeed for us who look back on those distant years, he ranks as a classic of the last pre-war period of Art from the very moment of his arrival in Paris.

His assimilation with Western art brought at the same time a freedom and a bondage to Chagall. The new powers of expression which he gained from outside sources set free his pictorial imagination in the happiest possible way, as is seen in his visions, in all that is calling in him for narration and description: the subjects he has cherished since childhood and the moments of new experience cognate with them. Freedom is also gained for the artistic idiom itself—a directness of utterance as characteristic of himself, as it is of the period. Chagall developes the optimum capabilities of the language of art and applies them to his purposes. He learns more and more that shapes, and above all, colours, have an autonomous life and an autonomous oppressivity and this is for him a veritable discov-

4

ery, although he is still limited in as far as the contents of his pictures is concerned. He now recognizes that beyond Naturalism he can enjoy a far greater freedom than he had ever dared hope for. This recognition frees him to accept every vision or expression that suggests itself to him.

At the same time his alliance to the Moderns bound him–submission to the rules of form recently declared paramount in Paris. No longer do we have naive, almost prenaturalistic principles of forming. From now on all is thought out and controlled. A strict adherence to form is imposed on every object. The movement of the figures no longer proceeds from within nor do they seem blindly and unresistingly to follow their destiny. All articulation and movement are dictated by Form. They are put together from surfaces and cubes, become crystalline structures and appear to be seen through prisms. And this is so down to the smallest details. Every shape now has a sharp-cut linear edge. The increased luminosity of the paints strengthens the effect of kaleidoscopic complexity. All this gives to Chagall's art a quite new character of consciousness and rationality. But it seems, at the same time, to have freed his utterance as never before.

If Chagall subscribes to the formal language, the Contemporary style of 1910, he does not offer a mere personal interpretation, to stand beside other interpretations of the Modernism of the period. With him the centre of gravity lies elsewhere. He does not even go the least distance along the road of " Abstract " art, not even in the hesitating manner which still allows an object to be the bearer of a formal experiment. In Chagall, however accentuated the formal aspect may be, it does not in the last resort have the decisive rôle. Intoxicated as he is by this newly acquired formal idiom and with whatever earnestness and eloquence he preaches it, it still means less for him than for those other artists, his new comrades and friends. He continues to be more concerned with the passionate realities of his subjects, which he can now treat in freer and ampler fashion thanks to the recently developed style.

He remains above all the story-teller. He has abandoned the ' genre ' manner of narration which he had practiced a few years earlier. Further, he is now dealing with tangible objects, in spite of their being fancy basically not fantastic, not far-fetched. If a cap is found floating at some distance from a head, or the head itself is apart from the trunk, the process remains a natural one. It is not the figment of a dream and implies no hallucination, but seems an everyday occurrence, highly natural and reported just as it happened; it need excite no more wonder than children feel for the most ordinary events. An adult would ask – " What is there to wonder at? " If he does not react in this natural way on viewing the picture, it is not due to anything unnatural in the picture but to the fact that the average eye is unaccustomed to such assumptions. Chagall may be a dreamer, but what he relates are not dreams but everyday events, lying wholly within the limits of what can be recounted. All these violations of spatial unity, distortion of objects and figures and contradictions of nature in whatever respect do not proceed from a revolutionary modernism but from Chagall's genuine, naive narrative fashion. They appear as simply as on Russian ikons or Persian miniatures, except that here it is the modern idiom which gives them such freedom of expression.

This manner of narration even at its most objective and palpable, is full of phantasy and dreaming. Chagall relates his dreams and dreams what he relates. There is no contradiction in this. Everything which has value for his senses has, both intrinsically the full importance of reality and at the same time the imponderability of a dream owing to the urge it evokes in the painter. Objects may fly through the air but they keep their solidity as objects. They are as tangible as real things but Chagall's spirit gives them the glamour of unreality.

The contrasts of real and unreal, rational and irrational do not find a place in Chagall's perception of the Universe nor in the primitiveness of his recital. We can only trace them in retrospect and thus establish the painter as a witness and forerunner of Surrealism, who thrives on these antitheses even when he strives to reject them. Chagall is not a Surrealist, he is a Realist through and through, devoted to all that is tangible, comprehensible and natural.

Among Chagall's most striking plastic methods is the apposition of objects and figures normally far apart in time and space. This has sometimes been regarded as a violation of reality. As if physical connections were more important to mankind than the spiritual. Are not countless distances in space bridged over in any story by the " And " of the narrator? Does he not leap over spacial continuity to preserve the intrinsic continuity of his tale? Chagall does just this. When he brings together in a picture two objects which have no contact in actual space, the procedure is natural and logical, for man is not only a living being—he is also a thinking and a feeling one. Thought and feeling overcome time and space. What Chagall depicts are not unnatural or supernatural events but the obvious realities of his soul, understandable to the everyday man.

Where he differs from all others who use the " modern " idiom is that, whether in the story-telling form of his earlier period or the lyrical manner of later years, he always has something to say. He has been called a Poet among Painters and his intimate friendship with poets and love of poetry seem to justify the title. Nevertheless he remains a painter through and through, the craftsman whose task is above all to produce good pictures. When he has a story to tell, he tells it in paint, just as the Early Christian legends were pictorially told. In both cases the story is what matters, but a story that lies only in the pictures and takes its strength of form from them. They may rightly be called Visions, in the identity of the image with the painting.

Meanwhile Chagall has had to abandon the style in which we· have considered him as a classic. The aspect through which he had viewed the world for a whole decade must be discarded if he was to trust wholly to his own eye. It was just as if he should discard a layer of skin. Much as the modern mode of vision had helped him to find his true self, from now on he must rely entirely on his own eyes. Most of the pictures of the classical period already give a subtle but expressive hint that the formal discipline to which he had bound himself was not suited to his true artistic nature. In nearly all of them we find, in places, particularly in living figures, many which are not included in the break-up of the prism but which follow peacefully the former, naive descriptive manner. They don't participate in the crystalline metamorphosis. Here we see quite clearly that with the cubist or «orphistic» construction an element of authenticity is lost.

Temperamentally, Chagall is not so much a strict, methodical draughtsman thinking in terms of rigid forms—he is much rather a painter. His element is free colour not line: line only finds justification in terms of objects and figures, where the scope of colour is limited. Chagall's first achievement, always within the bounds of his self-inflicted discipline, was to liberate colour and raise it to the finest enamel-like luminosity, so that the works even of his earliers period are triumphs of flowing colour. But in the end colour, in other words pure painting, had to shake off the shackles of form. This was achieved when Chagall's formal idiom towards the end of his first decade in Paris (and partly back in Russia) had acquired something "accentuated" over-sharpened, almost mannerised. But he overcame this phase and returned to his old self and created a new style. From then on he took his stand on pure colour. It is true that the figures and objects painted by him are not built only of colours, they have shapes as well. But he accepts their shapes somewhat passively and does not force them into pre-ordained moulds, stopping at an approximation to their appearance. It is once more the unquestioning presentation of his early period. But the forms are flattered by the ever blooming, ever happier tones. They atone for their stark objectivity and find rebirth in colour.

But now a surprising interruption takes place. In 1923 Chagall returns to Paris from the Russia of the first revolutionary years, to be met by an important offer from the art-dealer, Ambroise Vollard, for some illustrations. Chagall accepted and illustrated Gogol's "Dead Souls". A few years later, Vollard commissions him to illustrate the Fables of La Fontaine and in 1923 he begins his third great cycle—The Old Testament—which led him to visit the actual scenes of the Bible story. At the very moment when he was prepared to devote himself as a painter entirely to colour, Chagall became a draughtsman, and using colour most sparingly, he developed his new method of expression in just this field.

The pictures for a time appeared at longer intervals but there was no arrest in their flow, which soon became plentiful again. But the colour now—apart from the subject—is the chief means of expression—more than that, it carries the figures and objects and gives them existence. growth and the breath of life. He now builds up his picture, dividing it into areas according to colour rather than to any formal articulation. He cultivates every refinement of tone, making them bloom like flowers. No wonder that bouquets are now an ever recurring theme with him. In Russia, where they are almost unknown, bouquets had become the symbol of his beloved France, of childish innocence, of love—and, above all, of the idea of beauty in colour. Chagall's tones are now infused with a melting beauty. His pictures make a radiant, happy Sunday feast.

We have only to contrast these pictures with the work of his earlier period. The splendour of colour already revealed in those paintings is nevertheless a tinted surface. Even when the pictures are well-lighted, the effect remains without depth. The colours lie flat in the fashion of peasant art, a wonderful bloom on the picture. The colours don't decorate the picture, the pictures adorn themselves, with colours. Whereas in the later and last work, they seem to rise from the depths and to lose themselves once more in the depths. Chagall invents tones—a red, a green, a blue, a yellow, a violet—such as never existed before. They spring from an unknown root in which all colours are one, an eternal blackness which imparts a passionate glow to the colours that are wrung from it. Figures, till now palpable and firmly outlined, are bewitched by their coloration and recede into a distant miraculous zone. Chagall has become a great painter in the full sense of the word.

If we consider the subjects of these works, not much is altered. Lovers appear more often than before who have nothing to tell us but their love, and that in the language of colour. And there are also the docile domestic animals, the houses and churches of his childhood, but also the buildings, turrets and bridges of Paris—his " second Witebsk ". The old Jews, fiddlers with their fiddles, clocks and chandeliers, candles, torahs and crucifixes. These all testify

6

to the iconography of his heart and stand as symbols of his personal—yet not entirely private—world, miraculous but natural, never fantastic. The urge to tell a story changes to a lyrical fervour which no longer becomes dull, but which contemplates the real substance of men and objects, and the silent power of colour.

Meanwhile a darker period intervenes: the period of the apocalyptic persecution of his race, and the period of War. This gives birth to visions of crucifixions and Falling Angels, of burning villages and synagogues and suffering mankind—not in accusation but in endless lamentation, and yet filled with consolation—the consolation of true martyrdom.

And these are followed on an increased scale by dazzling visions of Life, especially pictures of Paris which now, as he takes up residence in the South of France on his return from overseas, rises like a phantom before his eyes, as once Witebsk had done. No one has sung this city in pictures as fully as Chagall in his last works.

But with all these changes, how little has really altered! Always the same faces arise, from his early work to his latest: cheerful faces, melancholy ones, the innocent and the knowing: they are all contemporary, whether they belong to men or animals. And there are always these warm, tender, sensitive hands that grip without gripping. Whether formed in cubist fashion or conventionally as in free hand painting they always give the same shy, sensitive, loving impression. One must love the painter for their sake if for naught else. Anyone not stirred by their song has failed to know him. They evoke our deepest, purest feeling without any overt appeal to them and no one need seek to resist this call.

Basel, 1956

CHRONOLOGY

1887   Born in Witebsk.

1907   Learns painting in a private art school in Witebsk.

1908   Petersburg. Attends the imperial art school. Meets Leon Bakst and works with him.

1910-14 Paris. Makes friends with the painters and men of letters: Blaise Cendrars, Canudo, Apollinaire, Max Jacob, and with the painters Fresnaye, Delaunay, Modigliani.

1914   Berlin. Exhibition of his paintings in the gallery "Der Sturm". Goes back to Witebsk.

1917   Russian Revolution. Appointed as Art Commissary of the Witebsk province. Founds there and directs an Academy of Art.

1919-22 Moscow. Paints frescoes for the Granowsky theatre. Writes his autobiography.

1922   Berlin. The first series of his etchings for "My Life" is published by Paul Cassirer. Paris.

1923   Charged by Ambroise Vollard to illustrate "The Dead Souls" by Gogol.

1924   First retrospective exhibition in the Barbazanges-Hodebert Gallery.

1926   First one man show in New York.

1927-30 Illustrates La Fontaine's "Fables" for Vollard.

1930   Begins to illustrate the Bible, for Vollard.

1931   Travels to Syria, Palestine, Egypt.

1932   Travels to Holland.

1933   Retrospective exhibition in the Kunsthalle, Basel.

1934   Travels to Spain.

1935   Travels to Poland.

1937   Travels to Italy.

1939   Beginning of the second world war. Goes to live in Gordes (South France).

1940   First prize of the Carnegie Foundation.

1941   Goes to the United States, invited by the Museum of Modern Art.

1942   Spends 3 months in Mexico. Draws scenes and costumes for the ballet "Aleko", music by Tschaikowsky.

1945   Draws scenes and costumes for the ballet "L'Oiseau de feu" by Stravinsky.

1946   Retrospective exhibition in the Museums of Modern Art in New York and Chicago.

1947   Paris. Retrospective exhibition in the Paris Museum of Modern Art, then in the Stedeljik Museum in Amsterdam, and in the Tate Gallery in London.

1948   International prize of Graphic Art of the XXIV Biennale in Venice.

1949   Goes to live in Vence. Works in ceramics. Paints frescoes for the foyer of the Watergate Theatre in London.

1951   Retrospective exhibitions in Zürich, Bern, New York.

1952   Travels to Greece. Exhibitions in Nice, Paris, New York.

1953   Exhibitions in Turin and Vienna.

1954   Travels to Greece. Exhibitions in Paris, Lüttich and Verwiers.

1955   Exhibitions in Houston (Texas) and Hanover.

1956   Exhibitions in Basel, Bern and Amsterdam.

1959   Exhibition Musée des Arts Décoratifs, Paris.

I

THE SABBATH

1909. Oil, 35⁷/₁₆″ × 37⁷/₁₆″. Wallraf-Richartz Museum, Cologne. Haubrich Collection.

Among the most impressive of Van Gogh's paintings is the " Night Café at Arles ". In a sleepless room bathed in glaring yellow light and in a perspective of strange insistence, a solitary figure stands by a vast billiard table, like a great black coffin. A few people are seated at the tables. In the choking silence one seems to hear the ticking of the clock on the wall: it alone marks the passage of time and every second is drawn out unbearably. Chagall's picture, painted in his early expressionist period before his encounter with the clarifying principles of cubism, recalls this work of Van Gogh.

The mood of the Sabbath evening is given expression with the same disquieting intensity. The figures sit, stand or lie about, under the oppressive glare of the oil-lamps, torpid with the dragging hours, marked again by a clock whose tick is almost audible, bowed down by the weight of their unbearable ennui. The holy candles, hals forgotten, stand uncompromisingly on the tables. We do not find Chagall's usual note in this work, but the scene was familiar to him from early childhood. The artistic idiom recalls the untaught style of the mourning scenes of simple people, but yet it goes beyond that in the power of its statement, the keen dissection of figures, space and objects, the sure touch in the grouping of the scene and, above all, the full, glowing, passionate colours. We have reached the completion of all that counts with Chagall: whatever further he has to relate is told in the direct utterance of the picture itself. He may be a story-teller, but he is above all a painter.

8

III

THE SOLDIER DRINKS

1912-13. Oil, 43″ × 37″. Museum of Modern Art, New York

It is only tea he is drinking, nothing stronger, and yet what a splendid intoxication he feels. For the tea that flows from the cherished samovar is the Elixir of Life, whose memory intoxicates the painter at his easel. The moustache is twisted high, the cap pushed back on the bald forehead. From the samovar's paunch flows not only fragrant tea but a comfortable, swaddling homely warmth. The block-house next door is seen through the window as it used to appear to the boy.

The crude awareness of the vision is increased by the stiff outlines of the figures. The technique, although appearing personal, is carefully studied, a cubism in colour chich nevertheless loses nothing of its sense of imagery. There is a full mastery of this idiom. The prismatic breakup does not permit the falling apart of the figures, the objects or of the composition. And the whole picture is intensified once more by the saturation of colour: The colours don't decorate the picture, the pictures adorn themselves, with colours like a work of peasant art.

All is methodical in this painting except the couple dancing, inspired by the warmth and comfort of the tea. They are not analysed cubistically, but on simple, naïve forms, which spring directly from the mood of the moment and at the same time recall in their guileless objectivity Chagall's work before he made contact with the art of Western Europe.

III

IV

THE VIOLINIST

1912-13. Oil, 74″×61″. Stedelijk Museum, Amsterdam

As a boy he had known this figure so well, the Jewish fiddler with his endless plaintive tones. He rises now gigantic in his memory, but still indigent, to conjure up against the dark background men, birds and gaily-coloured houses like an Orpheus hovering over the roofs of Vitebsk, nay over the whole globe, and all listen to his bitter-sweet, nostalgic notes. Mercy for the fiddler is assured by the holy figure that hovers benignantly overhead. And the painter shares directly in this blessing—for it is from him that we receive the heart-stirring message. With his only instruments—colour and form—he weaves a melody for us. If he is able to tell a story it is in the pure, clear language of the painting. The fiddler has no reality for us, other than his appearance in the picture. Tower, houses and trees—the snow itself—have no existence other than that the painter gives them. There is not a syllable here that is not spelt in the artist's own alphabet.

V

THE RABBI

1922-23. Oil, 46$^{1}/_{16}$″ × 35$^{1}/_{16}$″. Öffentliche Kunstsammlung, Basel

Leaning over the table, the boy fixes his awed gaze on the learned sage—wondering at his long beard, his crinkled locks, his dark outline. One cannot forget the child's unwavering look, not roaming as it well might over a thousand bright details, but held fast by the figure opposite. Everything it takes in is impressive—the book, the powerful hands—even the two meaningless buttons. All else is sunk in colour—yellow—common to table and ground, green flowing from the wall draperies to the green of the beard and wrinkled forehead. The sternness of his religion, softened by his humanity, is directed severely towards his observer, perhaps also on the artist himself, who was transgressing the law and the custom by the very act of painting the portrait.

VII

COCK AND HARLEQUIN

1928. Oil, 39³/₈″ × 31⁷/₁₆″. Private Collection, Paris

Here we no longer have the colouring of the earlier period, which clothed each object like a rich decoration or brightly hued skin and lay like a bloom on the painting. The surface is not so luminous as of old, but the picture in all its detail grows out of the element of colour. The colour is the creative material from which all life emanates and to which the ever-varied colours owe their existence. They glow from the depths and appear to be secretive and wonderful. The blue is not only air and water but is the endlessness of the colour. The green of the trees veils an endless mystery. The gaudy feathers in the bird's tail are full of magic poetry, like a sheaf of flowers brought by a lover. Even the red of the rider's trousers and the yellow of his jacket are suffused with light. The whole scene is born in colour and buried in colour. The Harlequin clings dreamily to the neck of his strange steed. The Cock limps stiffly and proudly along with its uncomprehended burden the object of caresses which leave it unmoved. It is satisfied with its beauty, feeling no need of any other love.

VIII

THE DESCENT OF THE ANGEL

1923-1933-1947. Oil, 58¹/₄″×65⁵/₁₆″. Offentliche Kunstsammlung, Basel

Chagall's work on this powerful picture covers a quarter of a century. He set about it three times before bringing it to completion. But more important than the time taken is the epoch of its conception—that historic moment that suddenly came to this planet also broke into Chagall's work. He does not give us a story or a real happening, but a vision of terror and enormous dramatic effect, a gesture from heaven rather than any human activity. A flaming angel plunges down on a peaceful world of roofs where men are living, a typical scene of oxen and violins, surrounded by religious tokens which rise warningly but at the same time reassuringly. This is not, like the other apocalyptic picture of the period— Picasso's "Guernica"—the angry cry of a stricken creature, it is not an exposition of man's cruelty, there is no accusation—only a plaint, an eternal martyrdom and lament, in which horror is banished by pity and faith. No bombs fall here to destroy mankind, only a dread flame in angelic form rends space for a second of time, while the symbols of Faith stand secure in Chagall's undestroyed, indestructible world: the fire has no power over them.

VIII. THE DESCENT OF THE ANGEL.

IX

THE RED SUN

1949. Oil, 55¹/₈″ × 39³/₄″. Collection of the Artist

Again and again in Chagall's pictures these couples appear—lovers, betrothed, newly-wed. They leave the ground and soar up in the heavens, the effusiveness of their feelings defying the law of gravity. So has he celebrated Love in countless paintings, countless re-groupings. He stands here almost unnoticed by the easel, his presence is hardly essential to the story. Before the red arc of the sun, the girl floats up in a dress of dreamy blue to meet her betrothed with his yellow suit, yellow face and green hair. The surrounding figures and objects share their joy—they are Chagall's returning symbols of his heart, the homely ox, the red cockerel, the three-armed chandelier and the flying violinist; and flowers, flowers. They spring from the dark background, gay because of their colours. No longer do the tones shade into one another as in his middle period—we have contrasts once more and defined edges, while colours are appropriate to their wearers and the picture is built on bold lines and balanced counterpoise. All this revives something of the breadth of his early work.

IX

X

SUNDAY

1953-54. Oil, 94⁷/₁₆″ × 82⁵/₈″. Collection of the Artist

"Sunday" is the title given by the artist to the great painting in which from the distant South he pays homage to his beloved city. All Chagall's work is redolent of Sunday, even when he handles the drabbest everyday theme. And many of his pictures are in a marriage mood like this one. Only the gloomy period of the martyrdom of this planet allowed visions of a different sort to cloud his outlook for a time.

Sunday reigns over the roofs and turrets of Paris. The broad front of Notre Dame, the soaring arrow of the Eiffel Tower, the bridges over the river, and faintly outlined a few houses rich in windows. Above this a sky which seems to reach further than that of any other city. It is also Sunday for the two lovers, whose heads brood like two great brows over the city, joined by flowing lines and also by a gently clasping hand, with the tenderest sheaf of flowers held in its slim fingers. One of his earlier pictures was "The Village and I", in which he told of faraway Vitebsk. Similarly, though in a different style of painting, Paris now calls to him from afar in his nostalgia. "The City and I". But even now his native village still holds a corner in his heart and therefore a corner of this picture.

He seems to have returned artistically to his great beginnings. Not a mere repetition, for he brings into play all that he has learned of freer, more advanced painting. But the picture is not a continuous area, but is divided in the older style into large, defined surfaces, with separate fields of colour. This work, like others of this period, is not only of vast dimensions, it is also immense in its vision. Its artistic and human fulfilment shows the greatness of the artist at this period.